GCSE **PE**
Revision Guide
AQA

Improving understanding through colour and clarity

Get your FREE digital book!

This book includes a free digital edition for use on a PC, Mac, tablet or smartphone.

Go to <u>ddedu.co.uk/pe</u>
and enter this code...

34XjEQShL

GCSE **Physical Education** AQA

Applied Anatomy and Physiology

The Skeleton	6 – 7
Joints	8 – 9
Muscles of the Body	10
How Muscles Work	11
The Respiratory System	12 – 13
The Cardiovascular System	14 – 15
Aerobic & Anaerobic Exercise	16 – 17
Effects of Exercise	18

Movement Analysis

Lever Systems	19
Planes & Axes of Movement	20 – 21

Physical Training

Fitness Testing	22
Agility	23
Balance	24
Cardiovascular Endurance	25
Coordination	26
Flexibility	27
Muscular Endurance	28
Power	29
Reaction Time	30
Strength	31
Speed	32
Principles of Training	33
Types of Training	34 – 35

Contents

Physical Training (continued)

Training Zones & Thresholds	36
Preventing Injuries	37
Training Seasons	38
Warm Up & Cool Down	39

Sport Psychology

Classification of Skills	40
Goals & Targets	41
Information Processing Model	42
Guidance	43
Mental Preparation	44
Personality	45

Socio-Cultural Influences

Influences on Participation	46
Commercialisation	47
Sporting Behaviour	48 – 49
Performance-Enhancing Drugs	50 – 51

Health, Fitness and Well-Being

Health, Fitness & Well-Being	52
Consequences of a Sedentary Lifestyle	53
Nutrition	54 – 55

Use of Data

Use of Data	56 – 57

THE SKELETON

There are more than 200 bones in the human body.

Cranium (skull)

Sternum (breastbone)

Scapula (shoulder blade)

Ribs (rib cage)

Vertebrae

Humerus (upper arm)

Pelvis

Ulna (forearm)

Radius (forearm)

Femur (thigh bone)

Tibia (shin bone)

Patella (kneecap)

Talus

Fibula (calf bone)

daydream EDUCATION

STRUCTURE OF THE SKELETON

The skeletal system works with the muscular system to allow movement at joints. The shape and type of bone at a joint determine the amount of movement.

Long Bones

Help translate the force generated by skeletal muscle into mechanical leverage; *e.g. femur.*

Flat Bones

Help protect the body's internal organs and with muscle attachment; *e.g. cranium and sternum.*

Short Bones

Help provide support and stability with little movement; *e.g. carpals and tarsals.*

FUNCTIONS OF THE SKELETON

Support

The skeleton supports the body. For example, a backbone enables us to stay upright.

Movement

The skeleton has joints where tendons join muscle to bone. This enables us to move. There are different types of joint that allow different types of movement.

Protection

The skeleton helps to protect vital internal organs from injury. For example, the cranium protects the brain.

Blood Cell Production

Blood cells are produced in bone marrow. Red cells transport oxygen, and white cells protect the body.

Mineral Storage

Important minerals, such as calcium and phosphorous, are stored in the bones.

Structural Shape and Points of Attachment

The skeleton provides a point of attachment for muscles. When muscles contract, they pull the bone to cause movement.

JOINTS

A joint is where two or more bones meet. There are three main types of joints:
- **Immovable** joints (e.g. skull) allow little or no movement.
- **Partially movable (cartilaginous)** joints (e.g. spine) allow a limited range of movement.
- **Freely movable (synovial)** joints (e.g. elbow, knee) allow free movement.

STRUCTURE OF A SYNOVIAL JOINT

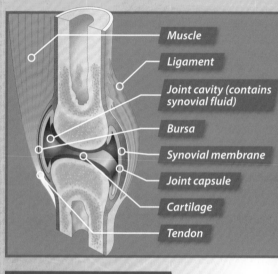

- Muscle
- Ligament
- Joint cavity (contains synovial fluid)
- Bursa
- Synovial membrane
- Joint capsule
- Cartilage
- Tendon

- Bones at freely movable (synovial) joints are held together by connective tissue.
- Ligaments are fibrous tissues that connect bones. They help keep joints stable.
- The ends of bones are covered in cartilage to aid movement, absorb shock and stop the bones from rubbing together.
- The joint capsule surrounds and seals the synovial joint and provides stability.
- The synovial membrane secretes synovial fluid into the joint cavity. This lubricates the joint and reduces friction.
- Bursae are fluid-filled sacs that reduce friction between bones and soft tissue, such as muscles or tendons.
- Tendons connect bones to muscles and enable movement.

TYPES OF SYNOVIAL JOINTS

Hinge

Hinge joints can be found at the elbow, knee and ankle. They provide movement in one plane for flexion and extension.

Example: enables flexion and extension at the elbow when performing a pull-up.

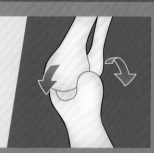

Ball and Socket

Ball and socket joints can be found at the hip and shoulder. They provide 360° rotation and movement in all planes for flexion, extension, abduction, adduction and rotation.

Example: enables rotation at the hip when hurdling.

8

daydream EDUCATION

RANGE OF MOVEMENT

Different types of joints allow different types of movement.

Rotation

*A turning or rotating movement around a **single axis**. This can occur at the shoulder.*

Extension

*When the angle at a joint **increases**. This can occur at the shoulder, elbow, hip and knee.*

Flexion

*When the angle at a joint **decreases**. This can occur at the shoulder, elbow, hip and knee.*

Abduction

*Movement **away** from the midline of the body. This can occur at the shoulder.*

Adduction

*Movement **towards** the midline of the body. This can occur at the shoulder.*

Plantar-Flexion

*Movement at the ankle joint that points the foot **downwards** away from the shin.*

Dorsi-Flexion

*Movement at the ankle joint that points the foot **upwards** towards the shin.*

MUSCLES OF THE BODY

Our muscles contract and relax to enable us to move. They also define body shape, protect internal organs, stabilise joints during movement and help maintain posture.

ANTERIOR

POSTERIOR

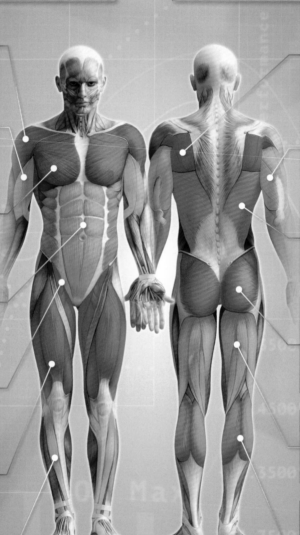

Deltoid
Abduction of the arm at the shoulder. **For example:** Bowling a cricket ball.

Biceps
Flexion of the arm at the elbow joint. **For example:** Pulling the paddle when kayaking.

Pectorals
Responsible for movement around the shoulder joint. **For example:** A chest pass in netball.

Abdominals
Flexion of the trunk and assisting with breathing. **For example:** A pike hold in gymnastics.

Hip Flexors
Flexion of the leg at the hip. **For example**: Driving out of the blocks at the start of a sprint.

Quadriceps
Extension of the leg at the knee joint. **For example:** Pushing the pedals when cycling.

Tibialis Anterior
Dorsiflexion of the ankle. **For example:** Lifting of the toes off the ground when walking and running.

Rotator Cuffs
Rotation and abduction of the shoulder. **For example:** Serving the ball in tennis.

Triceps
Extension of the arm at the elbow joint. **For example:** Throwing a javelin.

Latissimus Dorsi
Responsible for movement at the shoulder and lateral flexion of the spine. **For example:** Pulling the oars when rowing.

Gluteals
Responsible for movement of the leg around the hip. **For example:** Pushing your feet off the ground when sprinting.

Hamstring
Flexion of the leg at the knee joint. **For example:** Lifting your leg to kick a football.

Gastrocnemius
Flexion of the foot at the ankle joint and the leg at the knee joint. **For example:** Taking off when performing a high jump.

10

How Muscles Work

The human body contains more than 600 muscles.

ANTAGONISTIC MUSCLE PAIRS

Muscles contract to pull bones, but they cannot push them. Therefore, to achieve movement at joints, muscles work in pairs. These muscles are called antagonistic pairs. The muscle contracting is the agonist (prime mover) and the muscle relaxing is the antagonist.

The biceps and triceps are antagonistic muscles that work together to bend and straighten the arm.

Bending the Arm (flexion)

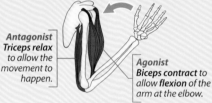

Antagonist Triceps relax to allow the movement to happen.

Agonist Biceps contract to allow **flexion** of the arm at the elbow.

Example: upward phase of a bicep curl

Straightening the Arm (extension)

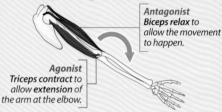

Antagonist Biceps relax to allow the movement to happen.

Agonist Triceps contract to allow **extension** of the arm at the elbow.

Example: downward phase of a bicep curl

The hamstrings and quadriceps are antagonistic muscles that work together to bend and straighten the leg.

Bending the Leg (flexion)

Agonist Hamstrings contract to allow **flexion** of the leg at the knee.

Antagonist Quadriceps relax to allow the movement to happen.

Example: bending the leg before kicking a ball

Straightening the Leg (extension)

Agonist Quadriceps contract to allow **extension** of the leg at the knee.

Antagonist Hamstrings relax to allow the movement to happen.

Example: straightening the leg to kick a ball

ISOMETRIC MUSCLE CONTRACTIONS

There is no change in joint angle and muscle length during isometric muscle contractions.

Example: performing a plank

ISOTONIC MUSCLE CONTRACTIONS

During isotonic muscle contractions, the muscle length changes as it contracts and causes movement. There are two types of contractions.

1 *Concentric*

Muscles shorten as muscle fibres contract.

Example: the upward (lifting) phase of a biceps curl

2 *Eccentric*

Muscles lengthen as muscle fibres contract.

Example: the downward (lowering) phase of a biceps curl

THE RESPIRATORY SYSTEM

*The **respiratory system** is the set of organs that is responsible for breathing: the movement of air in and out of the lungs. We breathe to draw oxygen into our bodies and expel carbon dioxide.*

THE PATHWAY OF AIR

1 Air passes through the nose or mouth and travels into the trachea.

2 The trachea divides into two tubes (bronchi), with one going to each lung.

3 The bronchi then split into smaller tubes (bronchioles).

4 The bronchioles end at the alveoli, where gaseous exchange takes place.

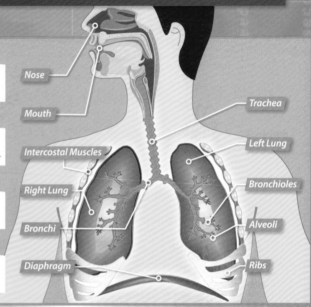

Nose — Trachea — Mouth — Left Lung — Intercostal Muscles — Bronchioles — Right Lung — Alveoli — Bronchi — Diaphragm — Ribs

GASEOUS EXCHANGE

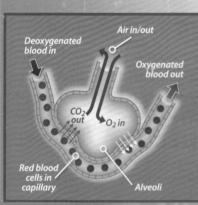

Deoxygenated blood in — Air in/out — Oxygenated blood out — CO_2 out — O_2 in — Red blood cells in capillary — Alveoli

Gaseous exchange occurs through a passive process called **diffusion**, in which gases move from an area of higher concentration to an area of lower concentration.

1 *Oxygen diffuses from the alveoli into the blood.*

2 *The oxygen combines with haemoglobin in the red blood cells to form oxyhaemoglobin.*

3 *Oxyhaemoglobin is carried to the muscles.*

4 *Haemoglobin carries the carbon dioxide produced in the tissue to the lungs, where it is removed from the body.*

FEATURES THAT ASSIST IN GASEOUS EXCHANGE

There are millions of alveoli in the lungs that, combined, provide a large surface area.	*Alveoli walls are moist and thin (only one cell thick) providing a thin permeable surface.*	*There is only a short distance for diffusion between the alveoli and the capillaries.*	*There are lots of capillaries around the alveoli that provide a large blood supply for gas exchange.*

daydream EDUCATION

THE MECHANICS OF BREATHING

Changes in air pressure between the atmosphere and the lungs cause the inhalation and exhalation of air.

Inhaling (Inspiration)

We inhale to supply our cells with oxygen.

AIR IN
21% Oxygen
0.04% Carbon Dioxide

Chest volume increases as air is sucked into the lungs.

The intercostal muscles contract to expand the rib cage.

The diaphragm contracts and moves down.

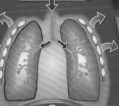

Exhaling (Expiration)

We exhale to remove carbon dioxide from our bodies.

AIR OUT
16% Oxygen
4% Carbon Dioxide

Chest volume decreases as air is forced out of the lungs.

The intercostal muscles relax to lower the rib cage.

The diaphragm relaxes and moves up.

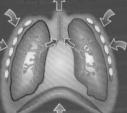

During exercise, the processes of inspiration and expiration are helped by other muscles.

Inspiration

*The additional contractions of the **pectoral** and **sternocleidomastoid** muscles allow more air to enter the lungs.*

Expiration

*The additional contraction of the **abdominal muscles** pulls the rib cage down faster, forcing the air out at a quicker speed.*

SPIROMETER TRACES

A **spirometer** measures lung volume, and produces a graph called a **spirometer trace**.

Spirometer Trace at Rest

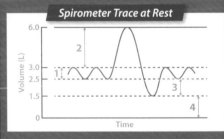

1 **Tidal Volume:** The volume of air normally inhaled and exhaled per breath.

2 **Inspiratory Reserve Volume:** The additional amount of air that can be inhaled (above tidal volume).

3 **Expiratory Reserve Volume:** The additional amount of air that can be exhaled (beyond tidal volume).

4 **Residual Volume:** The amount of air left in the lungs after maximal exhalation.

Spirometer Trace During Exercise

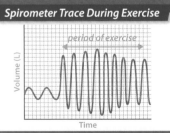

When you exercise, tidal volume increases as you take deeper breaths and breathing rate increases as you breathe more quickly.

As a result, the trace peaks and troughs get higher and lower respectively, and closer together.

THE CARDIOVASCULAR SYSTEM

The **cardiovascular system** consists of blood vessels and the heart. It is responsible for circulating blood and transporting oxygen, carbon dioxide and nutrients around your body.

STRUCTURE OF THE HEART

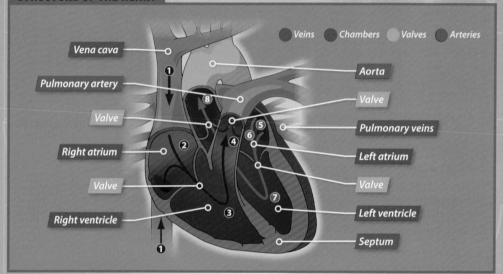

Veins • Chambers • Valves • Arteries

Vena cava

Pulmonary artery

Valve

Right atrium

Valve

Right ventricle

Aorta

Valve

Pulmonary veins

Left atrium

Valve

Left ventricle

Septum

THE CARDIAC CYCLE

The cardiac cycle is the sequence of events that occurs when the **heart** beats. There are two phases: **diastole** – when the chambers relax and fill with blood, and **systole** – when the chambers contract and eject blood.

1 Deoxygenated blood from the body is carried into the right atrium.

2 The right atrium contracts, pushing blood into the right ventricle.

3 The right ventricle contracts, pushing blood into the pulmonary artery.

4 The pulmonary artery transports deoxygenated blood to the lungs, where gas exchange occurs.

5 Oxygenated blood from the lungs is carried by the pulmonary veins into the left atrium.

6 The left atrium contracts, pushing blood into the left ventricle.

7 The left ventricle contracts, pushing blood into the aorta.

8 The aorta transports oxygenated blood to the body.

During the cardiac cycle, the heart valves open because of the pressure of blood and close to prevent backflow.

daydream EDUCATION

THE REDISTRIBUTION OF BLOOD DURING EXERCISE

During physical activity, blood is redistributed to both increase blood flow to and provide more oxygen for working muscles.

Vasodilation

Blood vessels leading to the working muscles open (dilate) to increase blood flow.

Vasoconstriction

Blood vessels leading to the digestive system close (constrict) to reduce blood flow.

THE BLOOD VESSELS

Arteries	Veins	Capillaries
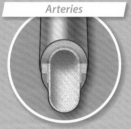	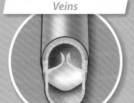	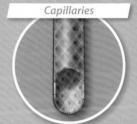

- Carry oxygenated blood (except pulmonary artery) at high pressure, from the heart to the body
- Have thick walls made of elastic fibres
- Have narrow channels (lumen) to maintain high pressure

- Carry deoxygenated blood (except pulmonary veins) at low pressure, from the body to the heart
- Have thin walls and contain valves to prevent backflow
- Have wide channels (lumen) to ease the flow of blood

- Allow the exchange of materials between tissues and blood
- Have walls that are only one cell thick
- Have channels (lumen) the width of one blood cell, which distort the cells and aid gaseous exchange

CARDIAC OUTPUT

Cardiac Output

The amount of blood pumped out of the left ventricle in one minute.

Stroke Volume

The amount of blood pumped out of the left ventricle in one contraction.

Heart Rate

The number of times the heart beats per minute.

Cardiac Output (Q) = Stroke Volume (SV) × Heart Rate (HR)

Cardiac output, stroke volume and heart rate all increase during exercise. This can be represented using a heart rate graph.

1 Heart rate is at its lowest point (resting heart rate) prior to exercise.

2 Just before exercise, heart rate increases (anticipatory rise).

3 As the intensity of exercise increases, heart rate increases.

4 The heart rate levels out as the level of intensity remains constant.

5 Heart rate drops quickly as exercise stops.

6 Heart rate returns to its resting level.

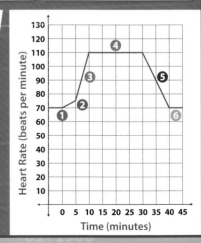

Aerobic & Anaerobic Exercise

AEROBIC EXERCISE

Aerobic exercise occurs in the presence of enough oxygen. During aerobic exercise, oxygen and glucose are used to create energy.

$$GLUCOSE + OXYGEN \longrightarrow ENERGY + CARBON\ DIOXIDE + WATER$$

Glucose is broken down to produce energy, carbon dioxide and water.

If there is insufficient oxygen for aerobic respiration, anaerobic respiration takes place.

SPORTING RELEVANCE

As long as your body has enough oxygen to meet the demands of your cells, your body will produce energy aerobically. Therefore, aerobic respiration is used in low- to medium-intensity activities, such as long-distance running, swimming, cycling and rowing.

Aerobic respiration is also essential for most individual and team sports, including dancing, boxing, basketball, hockey and squash.

ANAEROBIC EXERCISE

Anaerobic exercise occurs in the absence of enough oxygen. During anaerobic exercise, the body is unable to supply muscles with sufficient oxygen for aerobic exercise. It is represented by the following equation:

$$GLUCOSE \longrightarrow ENERGY + LACTIC\ ACID$$

Glucose is broken down to produce energy and lactic acid.

Anaerobic respiration produces approximately 5–10% of the energy that can be produced through aerobic respiration. Lactic acid can cause muscle pain and cramps.

daydream EDUCATION

Anaerobic respiration is used during intense exercises that require a short, sharp burst of effort.

Hockey	100m Sprint	Weightlifting	Javelin

Sprinting for a ball	Running 100 metres as fast as possible	Lifting a weight in one explosive movement	Throwing the javelin as far as possible

EPOC (OXYGEN DEBT) AND RECOVERY

After intense anaerobic exercise, extra oxygen is needed to convert lactic acid into waste products (carbon dioxide and water) that can be removed from the body. This is known as **EPOC** (Excess Post-Exercise Oxygen Consumption), or **oxygen debt**.

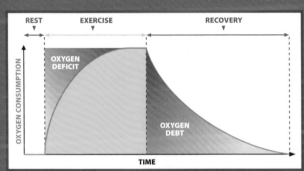

To facilitate this process we:

- Take deeper or quicker breaths to help with the intake of oxygen and removal of carbon dioxide.

- Perspire to lower the body's temperature and remove excess water through sweat.

- Excrete excess water and other waste products through urine and faeces.

A good cool-down will help with the breakdown and dispersal of lactic acid.

THE RECOVERY PROCESS

There are several methods that can be used to recover from vigorous exercise.

Rehydration	Manipulation of Diet	Massage	Ice Baths
Drinking plenty of water is vital to restore the fluids that have been lost during exercise.	Consuming carbohydrates will help to restore the glucose that has been used during exercise.	Massages increase blood flow, reduce inflammation and help to prevent delayed onset muscle soreness (DOMS).	Ice baths help to reduce inflammation and prevent DOMS by repairing the micro-tears that occur in muscle fibres.

Remember: An effective cool-down that involves stretching and light aerobic activity will help with recovery and the removal of lactic acid.

EFFECTS OF EXERCISE

Exercise has a range of effects on the body. These can be immediate, short-term or long-term.

IMMEDIATE (DURING EXERCISE)

During exercise, the working muscles require more oxygen and the following changes occur.

Increased Body Temperature
Skin becomes hot, sweaty and red as blood vessels near the skin open to allow heat to escape and cool the body.

Increased Breathing Rate
Depth and frequency of breathing speeds up to increase oxygen delivery and carbon dioxide removal.

Increased Heart Rate
Heart rate speeds up to increase blood flow to the working muscles and increase oxygen delivery and carbon dioxide removal.

SHORT-TERM (UP TO 36 HOURS AFTER EXERCISE)

Exercise can continue to affect the body for some time after an activity has been completed.

Fatigue
Tiredness and fatigue can occur because of low energy stores.

Light-Headedness
Light-headedness is usually a result of dehydration, low blood pressure or low energy stores.

Nausea
Nausea (a feeling of sickness) can be caused by overexertion or a lack of hydration.

DOMS
Aching, delayed onset muscle soreness (DOMS) and cramp can result from strenuous exercise.

LONG-TERM (AFTER MONTHS AND YEARS OF EXERCISE)

The adaptations that occur because of long-term exercise can bring about various benefits.

Change in Body Shape
Your body shape may change over time. This could include weight loss or an increase in muscle size.

Increase in Heart Size
The heart becomes bigger and stronger and can therefore pump more blood around the body.

Lower Resting Heart Rate (Bradycardia)
Resting heart rate decreases, and less recovery time is needed after exercise.

Depending on the type of physical activity, exercise can lead to improvements in specific components of fitness:

Muscle strength	Cardiovascular endurance	Muscular endurance
Speed	Flexibility	Stamina

daydream
EDUCATION

LEVER SYSTEMS

Muscles and bones work together to form **levers**. A lever is a rigid rod (usually a bone) that turns about a **pivot** (usually a joint). Levers can turn a small force into a bigger force. This is known as **mechanical advantage**.

If the fulcrum is closer to the effort than to the load, there will be a **mechanical disadvantage** and the output force will be less than the input force.

All levers are made up of three parts:

Effort
Input force

Fulcrum
Point about which the lever acts

Load
Opposing force

If the fulcrum is closer to the load than to the effort, there will be a **mechanical advantage** and the output force will be greater than the input force.

Mechanical Advantage = Effort Arm ÷ Weight (Load) Arm

FIRST-CLASS LEVERS

The fulcrum is positioned between the effort and the load.

When you lift your head to look up:

- The joint where your skull meets your spinal column acts as the fulcrum.
- The weight of your head is the load.
- The muscles at the top of your neck provide the effort to lift your head.

SECOND-CLASS LEVERS

The load is positioned between the fulcrum and the effort.

When you push off when jumping:

- The joints in your toes act as the fulcrum.
- The weight of your body is the load.
- Your calf muscles provide the effort to lift your body.

In this lever, the load is always closer to the fulcrum than the effort so there is always a **mechanical advantage**.

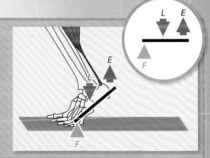

THIRD-CLASS LEVERS

The effort is positioned between the fulcrum and the load.

When you perform a biceps curl:

- Your elbow joint acts as the fulcrum.
- The weight of the dumbbell is the load.
- Your biceps provide the effort to lift the dumbbell.

In this lever, the effort is always closer to the fulcrum than the load so there is always a **mechanical disadvantage**.

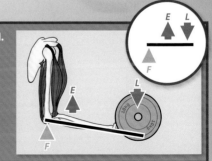

PLANES & AXES OF MOVEMENT

PLANES

Sagittal Plane
Runs vertically from front to back and divides the body into right and left parts.

Flexion and extension are movements in this plane. They are forward or backward movements parallel to the plane. Examples include a biceps curl, kicking a ball and running.

Movement **in the sagittal plane** takes place **about the frontal axis**.

Frontal Plane
Runs vertically from side to side and divides the body into anterior (front) and posterior (back) parts.

Abduction and adduction are movements in this plane. They are side movements parallel to the plane. Examples include a star jump, lateral raise and side lunge.

Movement **in the frontal plane** takes place **about the sagittal axis**.

Transverse Plane
Runs horizontally and divides the body into superior (top) and inferior (bottom) parts.

Rotation takes place in this plane. Examples include a golf swing, discus throw or wood-chop.

Movement **in the transverse plane** takes place **about the vertical axis**.

daydream EDUCATION

*Movement takes place **in a plane** and **about an axis**.*

Planes *- There are three imaginary planes that pass through the body to represent dynamic planes of movement.*

Axes *- An axis is a straight line around which an object rotates. There are three axes of rotation.*

AXES

Transverse Axis
Runs horizontally from side to side and is perpendicular to the sagittal plane.

A front or back somersault takes place in the sagittal plane about the transverse axis.

Sagittal Axis
Runs horizontally from front to back and is perpendicular to the frontal plane.

A cartwheel takes place in the frontal plane about the sagittal axis.

Longitudinal Axis
Runs vertically and is perpendicular to the transverse plane.

A 360° ice-skating spin takes place in the transverse plane about the longitudinal axis.

EXAMPLES

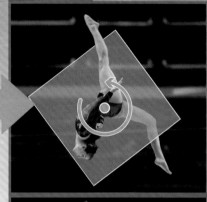

FITNESS TESTING

Fitness testing is used to measure the components of physical fitness.

REASONS FOR FITNESS TESTING

Fitness testing provides data that can determine your current fitness level and highlight strengths and weaknesses compared to normative data.

Fitness tests can be carried out before, during or after a training programme.

Before	Fitness test data can be used to show a starting level of fitness and to develop appropriate training requirements.
During	Fitness tests can provide variety to training and help you to monitor improvement, maintain motivation and set goals.
After	Fitness tests can help to determine the success of a training programme.

THE LIMITATIONS OF FITNESS TESTING

Fitness tests:

- *Can be too general and not sport-specific*
- *Do not include the movements of the actual activity*
- *Do not account for the competitive conditions of sports*
- *Take motivation to complete*

Some fitness tests can be inaccurate or unreliable as they do not use direct measuring. Many tests are also submaximal (less than the maximum of which a person is capable). An example of a submaximal fitness test is the Harvard Step Test.

It is important that fitness tests are always carried out with the correct procedures to increase validity.

FITNESS TESTING DATA

Data collected during fitness testing is **quantitative**; it has a numerical value and can be measured e.g. in seconds, levels, centimetres or numbers. Fitness test data can be compared against:

- *Your previous test scores*
- *The test scores of others in your class/group*
- *National averages (normative data)*

Qualitative data is described using words and cannot be measured. Qualitative data can be gathered through observation.

For example, a person who scored 10 cm on the Ruler Drop Test (quantitative), can make the observation that their reaction time is good, but not excellent; there's room for improvement (qualitative).

daydream
EDUCATION

AGILITY

Agility is the ability to *change direction quickly and accurately*, combining *speed, balance, power* and *coordination*. It is a *Skill-Related* component of physical fitness.

THE ILLINOIS AGILITY TEST

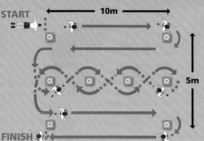

START — 10m
5m
FINISH

In the **Illinois Agility Test**, the participant runs a set route around a course as quickly as possible.

To complete the test, lie face down at the start cone and on the command 'go', jump up and complete the course (shown in the picture) as quickly as possible. Your score is based on the time (in seconds) it takes you to complete the course.

Normative data for the Illinois agility test is shown in the table below.

Gender	Age	Excellent	Good	Average	Fair	Poor
Male	16-19	<15.2	15.2-16.1	16.2-18.1	18.2-19.3	>19.3
Female	16-19	<17	17-17.9	18-21.7	21.8-23	>23

IMPROVING AGILITY

There are various training methods that can help improve agility. SAQ training and hurdle/ladder drills are great for improving speed, balance, power and coordination. Training can also be tailored to specific sports, for example, dribbling a football around a circuit as fast as possible.

SPORTING RELEVANCE

The ability to change direction quickly is required in most sports. Below are some examples of sporting activities in which good agility is essential.

Basketball | Rugby | Netball | Badminton

daydream
EDUCATION

BALANCE

Balance is the ability to **retain centre of mass** (gravity) above the base of support whilst stationary (static) or moving (dynamic). It is a **Skill-Related** component of physical fitness.

STORK TEST

The **Stork Test** measures **static balance**.

Stand with your hands on your hips, and place the sole of your right foot against the inside of your left knee, or vice versa. Rise up on the toes of your standing leg, and hold your balance for as long as possible. Record your time in seconds.

Normative data for the stork test is shown in the table below.

Gender	Age	Excellent	Good	Average	Fair	Poor
Male	16 – 19	>50	49.9 – 40	39.9 – 30	29.9 – 20	<20
Female	16 – 19	>30	29.9 – 23	22.9 – 16	15.9 – 10	<10

IMPROVING BALANCE

There are various training methods that can help improve static and dynamic balance, including SAQ training and hurdle/ladder drills.

Training your core muscles will also help you improve muscular balance. Try performing exercises on an exercise ball or bosu ball.

SPORTING RELEVANCE

Balance is a key attribute in most sports, from simple actions such as running to more complex activities such as gymnastics.

| Gymnastics | Skiing | Dance | Discus |

24

daydream EDUCATION

CARDIOVASCULAR ENDURANCE

Cardiovascular Endurance (aerobic power) is the ability of the heart and lungs to supply oxygen to the working muscles. It enables performers to exercise for prolonged periods of time, without tiring. It is a Health-Related component of physical fitness.

The cardiovascular system, which consists of the heart (cardio) and blood vessels (vascular) circulates blood around the body to deliver oxygen for energy production.

MULTI STAGE FITNESS TEST (MSFT)

This test entails running back and forth between 2 cones (20 metres apart) to a recording of timed bleeps that get increasingly faster.

You must keep running in time with the bleeps for as long as possible.

After you have finished, compare your result to the normative data for the MSFT below. The higher the level and number of shuttles completed, the better your cardiovascular endurance.

Age	Excellent	Good	Average	Fair	Poor
Male					
14 – 16	L12 S7	L11 S2	L8 S9	L7 S1	< L6 S6
17 – 20	L12 S12	L11 S6	L9 S2	L7 S6	< L7 S3
Female					
14 – 16	L10 S9	L9 S1	L6 S7	L5 S1	< L4 S7
17 – 20	L10 S11	L9 S3	L6 S8	L5 S2	< L4 S9

IMPROVING YOUR CARDIOVASCULAR FITNESS

You can improve your cardiovascular fitness by working in your aerobic training zone. This is found between 60% and 80% of your **maximum heart rate** (MHR = 220 – age).

You should exercise in this zone for at least 20 minutes. However, timing will vary depending on your fitness level and training goals.

Continuous, fartlek and circuit training are good methods for helping improve cardiovascular fitness.

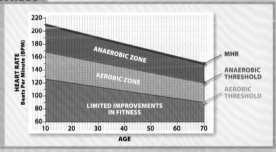

SPORTING RELEVANCE

Cardiovascular endurance is essential for sports that involve **prolonged periods of exercise**, such as long-distance running, swimming, cycling and rowing. It is also essential for most individual and team sports, including dancing, boxing, basketball, rugby and squash.

COORDINATION

Coordination is the ability to use a **combination of body parts and senses** at the same time to produce smooth and efficient movements. It is a **Skill-Related** component of physical fitness.

WALL TOSS TEST

The **Wall Toss Test** measures hand-eye coordination.

To perform the test, stand two metres from a wall, throw a ball against the wall with one hand and catch it with your other hand. Repeat this with alternate hands and record the number of successful catches in 30 seconds.

Normative data for the wall toss test is shown in the table below.

Excellent	Good	Average	Fair	Poor
>35	34 – 31	30 – 25	24 – 20	<20

IMPROVING COORDINATION

Coordination and motor skills form the basis of all sports. Fine motor skills involve small, precise movements, such as a snooker shot, whereas gross motor skills involve large muscle movements, such as a triple jump. Both types of motor skills can be improved through practice and training.

Ladder drills are a great way of improving coordination and agility.

SPORTING RELEVANCE

Most sports require a degree of coordination. Good coordination will help improve performance.

Hockey	Squash	Netball	Football
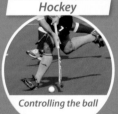			
Controlling the ball	Hitting the ball	Catching the ball	Dribbling the ball

daydream EDUCATION

FLEXIBILITY

Flexibility *is the range of movement around a joint. It is a* **Health-Related** *component of physical fitness.*

SIT AND REACH TEST

The **Sit and Reach Test** measures lower back and hamstring flexibility.

To perform this test, sit with your legs straight in front of you and the soles of your feet against the box. Reach forward as far as you can, hold for three seconds and record the distance reached in centimetres.

Normative data for the sit and reach test is shown in the table below.

Gender	Age	Excellent	Good	Average	Fair	Poor
Male	16-19	>14	14-11	10.9-7	6.9-4	<4
Female	16-19	>15	15-12	11.9-7	6.9-4	<4

IMPROVING FLEXIBILITY

You can improve your flexibility through **static and dynamic stretching**. Stretching improves range of movement, reduces the chance of injury and helps enhance performance. Therefore, it should play an important part in any training programme, warm-up and cool-down.

SPORTING RELEVANCE

Flexibility is needed in most sporting activities, in particular gymnastics and dance. Below are some examples of sporting activities in which **good flexibility** is vital.

Tennis Serve	Hurdles	Gymnastic Splits	Swimming

Shoulders & arms   Hips & legs   Hips & legs   Shoulders & arms

daydream EDUCATION

MUSCULAR ENDURANCE

Muscular Endurance is the ability of a voluntary muscle group or muscle to **work for a prolonged period of time without tiring**. It is a Health-Related component of physical fitness.

SIT-UP BLEEP TEST

This test entails performing sit-ups in time to beeps, which are set to a speed of 20 beeps per minute.

You must perform as many sit-ups as possible until you are unable to keep in time with the beeps.

The number of sit-ups completed is your score.

Normative data for the sit-up bleep test is shown in the table below.

Gender	Age	Excellent	Good	Average	Fair	Poor
Male	16 – 19	>55	55 – 40	39.9 – 30	29.9 – 20	<20
Female	16 – 19	>45	45 – 35	34.9 – 25	24.9 – 15	<15

IMPROVING YOUR MUSCULAR ENDURANCE

You can improve your muscular endurance by training your muscles to exercise for longer periods of time.

Circuit, fartlek and weight training are all great types of training that can help improve muscular endurance.

SPORTING RELEVANCE

Muscular endurance is needed in a huge variety of sporting activities. In addition to long-distance events such as running, swimming, rowing and cycling, muscular endurance is a key attribute in many team and individual sports such as football, netball, tennis and skiing.

Swimming

Cycling

Boxing

Rowing

daydream EDUCATION

POWER

Power, or explosive strength, is the **combination of explosive strength and speed of movement**. To generate power, you need good balance and coordination. Power is a **Skill-Related** component of physical fitness.

VERTICAL JUMP TEST

① ② ③

The **Vertical Jump Test** measures leg power.

To perform the test, stand side on to a wall, reach up as far as you can with your hand closest to the wall and mark your standing reach height. Then, driving with your arms and legs, jump as high as you can and touch the wall at the highest point.

The difference between your standing and jumping reach heights in centimetres is your score.

Normative data for the vertical jump test is shown in the table below.

Gender	Age	Excellent	Good	Average	Fair	Poor
Male	16 – 19	>65	65 – 50	49.9 – 40	39.9 – 30	<30
	>19	>70	70 – 56	55.9 – 41	40.9 – 30	<30
Female	16 – 19	>58	58 – 47	46.9 – 36	35.9 – 26	<26
	>19	>60	60 – 46	45.9 – 31	30.9 – 20	<20

IMPROVING POWER

You can improve power through training that involves explosive and dynamic movements, such as plyometrics or weight training using heavy weights and low repetitions.

SPORTING RELEVANCE

Most sports require a degree of power, and increasing your power can help improve performance.

Football	Baseball	Javelin	Weightlifting

Kicking the ball *Hitting the ball* *Throwing the javelin* *Pressing the weight*

REACTION TIME

*Reaction Time is the **time taken** to react to a **stimulus**. It is a **Skill-Related** component of physical fitness.*

RULER DROP TEST

The **Ruler Drop Test** measures reaction time. The test is performed with a partner who holds the ruler.

As your partner holds the ruler, stand with your hand in front of you and position the ruler in-between your index finger and thumb. The top of your index finger should be level with 0 cms on the ruler.

Your partner then drops the ruler, and you must catch the ruler as quickly as possible. Measure the point at which you caught the ruler from the top of your thumb. Repeat two more times, and then take an average of your three scores.

Normative data for the ruler drop test is shown in the table below.

Excellent	Good	Average	Fair	Poor
<7.5	<16	<20	<28	>28

IMPROVING REACTION TIME

Reaction time is an intrinsic skill. However, it can be improved through practice. For example, a sprinter can practise reacting to a starting pistol, or a football goalkeeper can practise reacting to a shot. Reaction time can also be improved by reading the situation and anticipating the stimuli.

SPORTING RELEVANCE

The ability to react quickly to a stimulus is required in most sports.

Cricket

A batsman reacting to a quick bowl

Table Tennis

A player reacting to a serve

Football

A goalkeeper reacting to a shot

Rugby

A player reacting to a sidestep

daydream EDUCATION

STRENGTH

Strength involves applying a **force** to overcome a resistance. It is a **Health-Related** component of physical fitness.

There are four main types of **Muscular Strength:**

Static	Dynamic	Explosive	Maximal
To apply a force to a fixed object. Muscle length stays the same (isometric contraction).	To repeatedly apply a force over a sustained period. Muscle length alters frequently over a period of time.	To apply a force in one fast movement. Muscles contract at a high speed.	To apply the maximum force possible in a single contraction. Muscle length changes (isotonic contraction).

HAND GRIP DYNAMOMETER TEST

This test involves squeezing the dynamometer grips together with maximum effort, and measures forearm and hand strength. Normative data for the hand grip test is shown in the table below.

Gender	Age	Excellent	Good	Average	Fair	Poor
Male	16-19	>56	56-51	50.9-45	44.9-39	<39
Female	16-19	>36	36-31	30.9-25	24.9-19	<19

IMPROVING MUSCULAR STRENGTH

Weight training is a great way to improve muscular strength. Below is a simple three-day training programme for improving overall strength. Aim to perform 3-4 sets of 4-8 reps at 70% of your 1-rep max for each exercise.

Day	Body Parts	Exercise 1	Exercise 2	Exercise 3	Exercise 4
1	Chest, triceps, shoulders	Bench press /Press-ups	Dumbbell flys	Shoulder press	Triceps extensions/Dips
2	Back, biceps, abdominals	Lat pulldowns/ Pull-ups	Biceps curls	Seated rows	Crunches/Leg raises/V-sits
3	Legs	Squats	Lunges	Leg press	Calf raises

To test maximal strength, the One-Rep Max Test can be used. It includes lifting the maximum weight you can in one attempt (kg), then comparing your results to a rating chart.

SPORTING RELEVANCE

Static	Dynamic	Explosive	Maximal

A rugby scrum Handstand Tug of war	Cycling Rock climbing Swimming	Shot-put Throwing a ball Discus	Power lifting Boxing

SPEED

*Speed is the ability to **move your body, or part of your body, quickly.** It is a **Skill-Related** component of physical fitness.*

30-METRE SPRINT

The **30-Metre Sprint** is used to measure maximum sprint speed.

It involves running 30 metres as fast as possible, with a rolling start (already running). Time is recorded in seconds.

Normative data for the 30-metre sprint test (in seconds) is shown in the table below.

Gender	Age	Excellent	Good	Average	Fair	Poor
Male	16 – 19	<4	4 – 4.2	4.21 – 4.4	4.41 – 4.6	>4.6
Female	16 – 19	<4	4 – 4.6	4.61 – 4.8	4.81 – 5	>5.0

Once your time has been recorded, you can calculate your speed in metres per second.

Your time: 4.4 $\dfrac{\text{Distance}}{\text{Time}} = \dfrac{30\text{ m}}{4.4\text{ s}}$ Your speed: 6.82 m/s

IMPROVING SPEED

Speed can be improved through training methods that concentrate on strength, power and technique.

Video analysis and practising the activity will improve technique, whereas interval, weight and plyometric training will improve strength and power.

Flexibility training can also help improve speed by increasing the range of movement of joints.

SPORTING RELEVANCE

Speed is essential in sport, especially for racing. However, it is also needed for specific movements. For example, cricket bowlers need to move their arms fast to bowl the ball as quickly as possible.

Boxing	Rugby	Javelin	Hockey

Throwing a punch

Racing for a ball

Throwing the javelin

Chasing after a ball

daydream EDUCATION

PRINCIPLES OF TRAINING

Training should be matched to the individual needs of the performer. When designing a training programme, the SPORT principles of training should be applied.

S — SPECIFICITY

Training programmes must be specific to the chosen activity.

Tailoring training programmes to the needs of performers will ensure that they train the correct muscles and body systems for their chosen activity. For example, the training needs of a marathon runner will differ from those of a weightlifter.

P O — PROGRESSIVE OVERLOAD

To improve and to continue to develop, a training programme must gradually be made more difficult.

As a performer becomes fitter, his or her training programme needs to be made more difficult to ensure fitness gains continue.

The increase in intensity must be gradual because increasing the intensity too quickly can increase the risk of injury.

R — REVERSIBILITY

Exercise improves fitness. Fitness levels drop if regular exercise is stopped.

If you train, your muscles get bigger (hypertrophy). Alternatively, if you stop training, your muscles get smaller (atrophy).

Although rest periods are an essential element of recovery, extended rest periods result in a reduction of physical fitness at a rate much higher than it was achieved. If you don't use it, you lose it!

T — TEDIUM

Training is a gradual process that can become tedious over time.

Using a variety of training methods will help you to stay motivated and avoid boring, repetitive training sessions.

KEY PRINCIPLES OF OVERLOAD

FITT

To become fitter, you must progressively work your body harder than normal. This can be achieved by applying the FITT principles.

Frequency – how often you exercise

Intensity – how hard you exercise

Time – how long you exercise

Type – how your training matches your chosen activity

TYPES OF TRAINING

Different training methods are suited to different sports and activities. As a result, sports performers must select training methods that suit, or can be adapted, to their chosen activity.

CIRCUIT

A series of exercises performed in a circuit that can be adapted to suit most sports.

Excellent for general fitness; can also incorporate skills, such as passing or dribbling a ball in basketball or football.

+ Develops both aerobic and anaerobic systems
+ The content/demand of the circuit can be adapted to suit specific sports and improve different components of fitness
+ Easy to monitor work rate and progression

− Can require lots of space, equipment and time to set up (typically 6-12 circuit stations)
− Can be difficult to maintain work rate

CONTINUOUS

Involves sustained exercise at a constant rate (steady state) without rests. The performer works aerobically for at least 20 minutes.

Suitable for endurance events such as middle- and long-distance running, cycling or swimming.

+ Improves aerobic fitness, cardiovascular fitness and muscular endurance
+ Easy to monitor work rate and progression
+ Limited equipment or facilities required

− Does not develop other components of fitness
− Time-consuming
− Can become repetitive and boring

FARTLEK (SPEED PLAY)

A continuous workout involving changes in speed and/or terrain.

Suitable for sports involving constant changes in intensity, such as netball, rugby, hockey and basketball.

+ Develops both aerobic and anaerobic systems
+ Improves cardiovascular fitness and muscular endurance
+ Can be adapted to suit most sports and improve other components of fitness

− Can become repetitive and boring
− Difficult to monitor work rate and progression
− Can be difficult to maintain work rate

INTERVAL

Involves alternating periods of work and rest.

Suitable for sports involving alternating periods of intense effort and rest, such as basketball, rugby, hockey and netball.

+ Develops both aerobic and anaerobic systems
+ Can be adapted to suit specific sports and improve other components of fitness
+ Easy to monitor work rate and progression

− Can become repetitive and boring
− Can be difficult to maintain work rate

daydream EDUCATION

WEIGHT TRAINING

A type of interval training that involves using weights as a form of resistance. The choice of weight/exercise will depend on your fitness aim.

Suitable for all activities, especially those involving power and strength, such as shot-put, sprinting, rugby and wrestling.

+ Improves muscular strength, endurance, size and power
+ High reps, low weight for muscular endurance
+ Low reps, high weight for strength and power
+ Easy to monitor work rate and progression

− Requires specialist equipment
− Can cause serious injury if incorrect techniques are used; safe practice, the correct lifting techniques and spotters are all important

PLYOMETRICS

Exercises in which muscles exert maximum force in short intervals of time, with the goal of increasing power. While bounding, an eccentric contraction is followed by a larger concentric contraction.

Suitable for activities that require explosive strength and power, such as sprinting, track and field events, football and rugby.

+ Improves muscular strength, power and speed
+ Can utilize the whole body
+ No equipment required

− Very demanding on muscles and joints
− High risk of injury

STATIC STRETCHING

Involves holding a stretch (isometric) for up to 30 seconds. Commonly used in warm-ups and cool-downs but can also be a training type.

Suitable for all activities, especially those requiring an increase in range of movement, such as dancing, gymnastics and hurdling.

+ Increases flexibility
+ Can be relaxing

− Can be time-consuming
− Some muscles are difficult to stretch

When performing stretches, it is important to avoid overstretching.

HIGH-ALTITUDE TRAINING

High-altitude training is an aerobic training technique that involves training at high altitude (2000 m above sea level).

There is less oxygen in the air at high altitude. The body's oxygen carrying capacity is reduced.

The body adapts by making more red blood cells to carry oxygen to muscles and organs.

As the body has a higher red blood cell count, cardiovascular endurance at a lower altitude may improve.

+ Improves cardiovascular and muscular endurance which benefits aerobic athletes, e.g. marathon runners

− Little benefit for anaerobic athletes, e.g. 100 m sprinters
− Travel to training areas can be expensive
− Altitude sickness
− Effects only last for a limited time

Remember: Any training must take account of the training purposes, the training thresholds, targets and zones and the work:rest ratio.

TRAINING ZONES & THRESHOLDS

By understanding training zones and thresholds, sports performers can ensure that they train at the correct intensity to work the desired energy system. This helps them create specific training programmes that match their goals.

MONITORING HEART RATE

Training zones and thresholds are determined by percentages of **maximum heart rate (MHR)** which can be calculated using the following formula:

MAXIMUM HEART RATE = 220 – YOUR AGE

The most accurate way to measure your heart rate is with a heart rate monitor. Alternatively, you can measure it manually by finding your pulse in your wrist or neck and counting the number of times your heart beats in one minute.

TRAINING THRESHOLDS

Training zones and thresholds are determined by percentage of MHR.

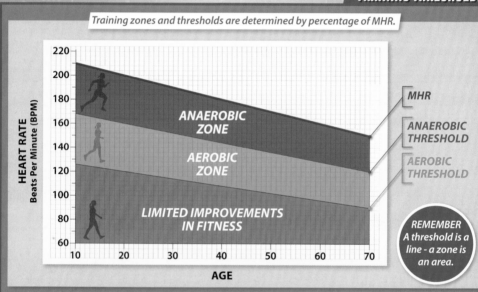

REMEMBER
A threshold is a line - a zone is an area.

Zone	Intensity	% of MHR	Why train in this zone	Examples
Anaerobic	High to Very High	80-90%	Anaerobic activity promotes strength, speed and power, and improves the body's ability to dispose of lactic acid. Training time is short because of the high intensity.	Activities that require all-out effort such as weightlifting and sprinting.
Aerobic	Light to Moderate	60-80%	Aerobic activity improves cardiovascular fitness and aerobic capacity. The aerobic energy system can work for long periods.	Long-distance swimming, jogging and rowing.
Limited Improvement	Very Light	Below 60%	Training below the aerobic threshold results in limited fitness improvements. You would train in this zone when first starting an exercise programme or warming up.	Gentle walk.

daydream
EDUCATION

PREVENTING INJURIES

To **optimise training** and **reduce the chance of injury**, training **type** and **intensity** should be **tailored** to meet the needs of the performer.

The following factors should be considered when undertaking physical activity to reduce the risk of injury.

WARM UP AND COOL DOWN

Always complete a full warm up and cool down.

AVOID OVERTRAINING

Avoid overtraining: don't train too often or too intensely.

CHOOSE APPROPRIATE KIT

Wear appropriate clothing and footwear. For example, football shin pads.

STAY HYDRATED

Drink plenty of water to avoid dehydration, which can increase the chance and effects of injury.

AVOID OVERSTRETCHING

Avoid overstretching muscles and bouncing when stretching.

USE CORRECT TECHNIQUE

Use correct techniques. For example, when lifting weights.

REST

Rest between training sessions and allow for recovery.

USE TAPE/BRACING AS NECESSARY

Tape or brace as necessary for extra support. For example, by wearing a brace to support a knee injury.

In addition to these precautions, it's important to ensure that the type and intensity of your training always match the training purpose.

TRAINING SEASONS

POST-SEASON/TRANSITION

Approximately 6-8 weeks

Fitness levels are maintained through light exercise. Performers build aerobic fitness and begin specific strength training. Some performers will also look to develop skill weaknesses identified during the peak season.

PRE-SEASON

Approximately 6-8 weeks

Performers build on their aerobic base (established in the off season) developing specific components of fitness, such as speed and power. Friendly matches are organised in preparation for the peak season.

A training year is divided into the following seasons/phases:

REST/RECUPERATION

Approximately 2 weeks

Following an intense peak season, performers will take a rest from training. During this time the body is able to recover from injuries. Often this period is combined with the off/closed season.

PEAK/PLAYING SEASON

Up to 40 weeks

With the emphasis on speed, skills are practised under pressure to simulate game play so strategies and tactics are perfected. Games are played once or twice a week and performers aim to maintain their pre-season fitness.

daydream EDUCATION

WARM UP & COOL DOWN

All exercise sessions, whether aerobic or anaerobic, should consist of a warm-up, a main exercise session and a cool-down.

WARM-UP

A warm-up safely prepares the body, physically and mentally, for more strenuous activity and reduces the likelihood of injury. Cool muscles do not absorb nutrients and oxygen or impact as well as warm muscles.

A warm-up should be specific to your chosen activity, and include the following:

A Pulse Raiser	Stretching	Skill-Based Practices	Mental Preparation

Raising your pulse through gentle aerobic activity will help increase your heart rate and body temperature.	Static and dynamic stretching helps improve range of movement, mobilise joints and maintain body temperature.	A warm-up should include activity specific drills, such as low-intensity golf swings or tennis serves.	Psychological preparation will help you to get focused and ready for the main session.

Warming up before a main exercise session will increase oxygen delivery to the working muscles, helping with the production of energy.

MAIN SESSION

The main session can be a training programme, a game or a match. If the main session is a training programme, it is vital to ensure it is tailored to meet your specific needs and incorporates the principles of training.

COOL-DOWN

An effective cool-down assists recovery, reduces heart rate and helps with the removal of lactic acid, CO_2 and other waste products. Like a warm-up, a cool-down should include light cardio exercise, such as a walk or jog, to maintain elevated breathing and heart rate.

A cool-down should also include stretching and a gradual reduction in intensity to decrease muscle tension and return muscles to a pre-exercise state, preventing the delayed onset of muscle soreness (DOMS).

CLASSIFICATION OF SKILLS

Skill is a **learned** action that brings about expected results. Ability is having the skill to do something.

Skills can be:

BASIC **OR** COMPLEX

BASIC
- Little information to process
- Few decisions to make
- Used in many sports

COMPLEX
- Lots of information to process
- Decisions need to be made quickly
- Generally sport specific

OPEN **OR** CLOSED

OPEN
- Affected by the environment
- Involve decision making
- Externally paced

CLOSED
- Not affected by the environment
- The skill is habitual
- Self-paced

SELF-PACED **OR** EXTERNALLY PACED

SELF-PACED
- Start time and pace controlled by the performer
- No external factors
- Usually closed skills

EXTERNALLY PACED
- Start time and pace controlled by the external environment
- Involves reacting to external factors
- Usually open skills

GROSS **OR** FINE

GROSS
- Large, powerful movements
- Performed by major muscle groups
- Not very precise

FINE
- Small, precise movements
- Performed by small muscle groups
- Requires high levels of hand eye coordination

daydream EDUCATION

GOALS & TARGETS

When you train, it is important to set goals and targets. Setting achievable goals and targets will help you to stay motivated and focused.

Performance Goals

Performance goals focus on personal performance.

Sporting example: *A swimmer aiming to beat their personal best time.*

Outcome Goals

Outcome goals focus on the end result: winning.

Sporting example: *A tennis player wanting to beat an opponent.*

Performance and outcome goals can be combined. However, it is generally accepted that outcome goals should be avoided, especially for beginners who may become demotivated by failure.

SMART TARGETS

The use of SMART targets when setting goals can help to improve and optimise performance.

S — SPECIFIC

Clearly explain what you want to achieve and ensure your target is specific and relevant.

✓ ***Specific –*** *I want to improve my pass completion percentage.*

✗ ***Vague –*** *I want to be better at hockey.*

M — MEASURABLE

Set measurable targets so you can track your progress and measure if your target has been achieved.

✓ ***Measurable –*** *I want to improve my 50-km time by five minutes.*

✗ ***Unmeasurable –*** *I want to be better at cycling.*

A — ACCEPTED

Any targets should be decided on by all participants.

✓ ***Accepted –*** *My coach and I agree that I need to improve my shooting accuracy by 10%.*

✗ ***Unaccepted –*** *I want my team to try harder.*

R — REALISTIC

Ensure your target is realistic for you personally. Factors, such as work and hobbies, affect your ability to meet your targets. As such, the second target below is likely to be unrealistic.

✓ ***Realistic –*** *I want to train three days a week.*

✗ ***Unrealistic –*** *I want to train seven days a week.*

T — TIME-BOUND

Create a timeframe for you to achieve your targets. Set an end point as a deadline for achieving your final goal. Establishing a timescale can also help you stay focused.

✓ ***Time-bound –*** *I want to beat my personal best (PB) within two months.*

✗ ***Not time-bound –*** *I want to improve my swimming.*

Having SMART targets will motivate you to stay on track!

*Always check that your targets are **SMART**!*

41

INFORMATION PROCESSING MODEL

The performance of a skill can be broken down into stages.

INPUT
Information from the senses about the environment (involves selective attention).

DECISION MAKING
Selection of appropriate response from memory.

OUTPUT
Information sent to muscles to carry out the response.

FEEDBACK
Information received about a performance. It can be positive or negative and can have a big impact on performance.

LONG-TERM MEMORY
Long-term memory is information that has been remembered for use in the future, e.g. the sequence of a dance routine.

SHORT-TERM MEMORY
Short-term memory is information that is only remembered for a matter of seconds, e.g. your teammate's position when passing a netball.

TYPES OF FEEDBACK

Intrinsic

Extrinsic

Intrinsic feedback is based on how a performance felt to the performer.
Experienced performers will know when something feels right or wrong, whereas beginners may not have such experience.

Extrinsic feedback comes from another person who saw the performance, such as a coach.
Beginners will benefit greatly from extrinsic feedback as they may not have the knowledge to assess their own performance.

+ *Positive feedback is focused on the things that went well in a performance. It is effective for beginners that may lack confidence and need encouragement.*

− *Negative feedback is focused on the things that need to be improved in a performance. It is more effective for experienced performers that need to perfect their performance.*

Feedback can focus on the technical performance or the results of a performance.

Knowledge of Performance (KP)
Examining the execution of the movements performed (technique) enables performers to assess the correctness of their movements. For example, a golfer watching a video of his or her last practice swing.

Knowledge of Result (KR)
Examining performance results enables performers to analyse their performance and compare it to previous performances. For example, race times in track events, pass completion rates in netball or tackles made in rugby.

Example: Football free kick
Input: *Goalkeeper positioned left, wall too far right, no wind.*
Decision Making: *Use experience and skill to determine where to kick the ball.*
Output: *Kick ball hard with dip into the top right corner of the goal.*
Feedback: *KR – no goal, too high; KP – felt good, more dip next time.*

daydream EDUCATION

GUIDANCE

There are four main types of guidance that are used to assist in the learning process.

VISUAL GUIDANCE

Practical demonstrations, diagrams and other visual prompts are used to help the learner create a mental image of the skill that needs to be learned.

+ Helps the learner visualise the skill
+ Can be used at all stages of learning but most effective at the early stages
+ Skills can be broken down into parts (sub-routines) to highlight the technical stages

− Must be accurate and technically correct
− Complex skills can be very difficult for a learner to comprehend
− Static visual aids may not provide enough guidance or information

VERBAL GUIDANCE

A spoken explanation of how a skill is performed is provided. It is often used with elite level performers.

+ Effective when used in conjunction with other forms of guidance
+ Good for elite level performers
+ Can be provided during a performance and is ideal for open skills

− Explanations must be clear and concise not to confuse the learner
− Must limit the amount of information
− Complex and high organisational skills are very difficult to explain verbally

MANUAL GUIDANCE

The teacher or coach physically moves the body of the learner through the correct pattern of movement. For example, a coach may guide a performer through a forehand tennis shot.

+ Can be used with learners of all abilities
+ Helps the learner gain a kinaesthetic sense of the movement
+ Helps build confidence

− The learner can become dependent on the guidance
− Difficult when working with large groups

MECHANICAL GUIDANCE

Equipment is used to help the learner practise a skill – for example, a new swimmer using a float.

+ Very effective for beginners
+ Helps the learner gain a kinaesthetic sense of the movement
+ Helps build confidence

− The learner can become dependent on the guidance
− The movement experienced with guidance may be different to the actual movement

MENTAL PREPARATION

In order to perform at the optimum level, you need to ensure that you are mentally prepared.

AROUSAL

Arousal refers to your level of excitement and readiness to perform.

If your arousal level is too low, you are not likely to be driven or motivated enough to perform at your optimum level.

If your arousal level is too high, you are likely to get nervous, anxious or over-aggressive.

Optimum arousal level varies for different sports.

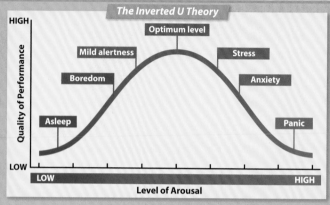

The Inverted U Theory

- HIGH / LOW (Quality of Performance)
- Optimum level
- Mild alertness
- Boredom
- Stress
- Anxiety
- Asleep
- Panic
- LOW — HIGH (Level of Arousal)

The optimum arousal level for sports that require fine motor skills, such as snooker, is relatively low. Conversely, the optimum arousal level for sports that require gross motor skills and aggression, such as rugby, is relatively high. Therefore, it is important to mentally prepare specifically for your chosen activity.

STRESS MANAGEMENT TECHNIQUES

Various mental preparation techniques can be used to help you reach optimum arousal level before a sporting activity.

1. Positive Self Talk *Using self talk and positive imagery to create a positive frame of mind.*

2. Mental Rehearsal *Visualise performing the activity or skill successfully to boost confidence.*

3. Deep Breathing *Stay calm and practise deep breathing to relax and reduce anxiety.*

MOTIVATION

Motivation is the ability and desire to initiate and persist at a task. It greatly affects performance and can be intrinsic (from within) or extrinsic (from another source or person).

Intrinsic

- Linked to pride, self-satisfaction & personal achievement
- Can lead to continued effort and participation
- Generally considered more effective than extrinsic motivation

Extrinsic

- Can be tangible; e.g. certificates/trophies, or intangible; e.g. praise/applause
- Extrinsic rewards can result in feelings of pride (intrinsic).
- Performers may become reliant on extrinsic motivation if overused.

Both intrinsic and extrinsic motivation are effective for success. However, unless you have the internal drive and desire to succeed, it can be difficult to remain motivated.

daydream EDUCATION

PERSONALITY

Personality is the combination of characteristics and qualities that form an individual's character.

INTROVERTS

Introverts are shy, quiet and thoughtful. They generally enjoy being on their own.

Introverts tend to prefer playing individual sports that require low arousal but high levels of concentration and precision (fine skill control).

Sporting examples include: archery, golf and snooker.

EXTROVERTS

Extroverts are enthusiastic, talkative and enjoy social interaction. They often become bored when alone and are aroused by others.

Extroverts tend to prefer playing team sports that are fast paced, require gross skills and may not need high levels of concentration.

Sporting examples include: rugby, football and basketball.

Most of us are somewhere in-between an introvert and an extrovert.

AGGRESSION

There are two main types of aggression: **direct** and **indirect**.

DIRECT AGGRESSION

Direct aggression is aimed directly at other players and involves physical contact. It can cause physical harm.

Sporting Relevance

A tackle in rugby to stop the player from running with the ball.

A punch in boxing.

INDIRECT AGGRESSION

Indirect aggression is aimed at an object to gain an advantage over an opponent. It can cause psychological harm.

Sporting Relevance

Bowling a bouncer in cricket to intimidate the batsman.

Smashing a shuttlecock hard to get it to the floor quicker and win the point.

daydream
EDUCATION

INFLUENCES ON PARTICIPATION

> Engagement patterns in sport can differ between different social groups.

PEOPLE

Family

Parents, siblings and other relatives may encourage you to take part in particular activities and offer financial and emotional support. Some people may find they have less available leisure time due to family commitments.

Peers

Friends, classmates and members of your sports club may encourage you to play the sports that interest them and avoid others. Good performers at your school or sports club can become role models and inspire you to compete in specific sports.

GENDER

Women's participation levels in sport are increasing. However, there are still fewer women participating in sport than men, particularly in football and golf. Biased media coverage, fewer opportunities and stereotyping are all blamed for this.

Men's sport dominates the media, with women's events receiving a much lower profile. This contributes to fewer opportunities and less funding for women and fewer female role models.

Some sports are also associated with either men or women (gender tagging). For example, some consider netball to be a feminine sport, and boxing to be a masculine sport. These perceptions can influence a person's decision to participate in a given sport.

RACE, RELIGION & CULTURE

Race, religious beliefs and culture can have a big impact on participation in sport.

Some religions have strict guidelines that may affect religious people's decision to participate in sport. For example, some Christians will not participate in sport on a Sunday.

Unfortunately, racism is still an issue in sport despite huge efforts to promote racial equality.

AGE

Age can affect a person's ability to participate in certain activities.

For example, weight lifting can be damaging to children, whereas physical sports, such as rugby, can be too demanding for elderly people. As a result, people of different ages will participate in different sports.

DISABILITY

A disability may affect a person's ability to participate in certain activities. However, many sports, such as basketball (wheelchair basketball), have been adapted to enable people with disabilities to participate.

Events such as the Paralympics have helped raise the profile of disabled sports.

There are other factors that affect engagement patterns in sport, including a person's socio-economic group, level of education and familiarity with the given sport.

daydream EDUCATION

COMMERCIALISATION

The commercialisation of sport involves the sale, display or use of sport to generate income.

Sport is a multibillion-pound industry, with sporting events and performers attracting huge media interest and sponsorship deals. Sports, the media and sponsors all benefit from, and are dependent on, one another.

Sport

Sports teams use the money to invest in facilities, players, coaches, provision and their own promotion. Companies sponsor sports teams, events and performers to promote their products to a wider audience and to enhance their image.

Types of sponsorship include finance, equipment and facilities.

Sports teams profit financially and benefit from increased awareness and exposure.

The media pays for the rights to broadcast sporting events.

Media coverage can inspire people to participate in sport.

Sponsorship

Media

The media, which includes television, radio, the Internet and the press, provides sponsors with a wider audience to promote their product or service to. This can result in greater sponsorship for sports.

	Effects of Commercialisation	Effects of Technology
Performers	+ Increased income + Better equipment & facilities − Loss of privacy & free time − Increased pressure to win	+ Improved performance, e.g. new bike parts making bikes quicker + Improved analysis − The latest technology is expensive − Can provide an unfair advantage
Sports	+ Increased awareness + Increased media coverage − Less funding for minority sports − Media can influence scheduling	+ Better facilities and security + Improved performance/entertainment − Technology can fail − May disrupt flow of play
Officials	+ Income and opportunities to travel − More scrutiny and negative publicity if officials make poor decisions	+ More accurate decision-making, e.g. Hawkeye in cricket and VAR in football − Potential for over-reliance on technology
Spectators	+ More coverage + Better equipment and facilities − Higher costs of attending events and merchandise	+ More viewing options, e.g. live online streaming and 'red button' option − High costs of TV subscription packages
Sponsors	+ Increased awareness and sales − Negative publicity if sponsored players or teams cheat, misbehave or perform badly	+ New opportunities for promotion and increased awareness − High costs of funding new technologies

SPORTING BEHAVIOUR

SPORTSMANSHIP

As well as having rules, sports often have unwritten codes of conduct that ensure players are honest and respectful to their opponents. This is known as *etiquette*.

Sportsmanship involves ethical, appropriate, polite and fair behaviour while participating in sporting activities.

Examples:
- *A cricketer 'walking' before officially being given out*
- *A footballer kicking the ball out of play when another player is injured*
- *Tennis players shaking hands at the end of a game*

The **contract to compete** is an unwritten code whereby performers agree to try their best, play by the rules and respect their competitors through good sportsmanship.

GAMESMANSHIP

Gamesmanship involves the use of 'unfair' tactics to gain an advantage in a sporting activity. It involves pushing the rules to the limit without breaking them. Therefore, it usually goes unpunished.

Examples:
- *Deliberately losing a game to get an 'easier' draw in a competition*
- *Wasting time to break up the flow of a game or run down the clock*
- *Faking an injury in any sporting activity*

DEVIANCE

Sporting deviance is behaviour that falls outside the laws of a sport or is deemed unacceptable. All sports have rules to discourage deviance, but due to the high-pressure nature of sport, it is still rife.

Examples of deviance include:

| Use of performance-enhancing drugs | Violence | Match fixing | Professional fouls |

Reasons for deviance:

| High pressure to win | Lack of moral constraint | Rewards of winning are too high | "Win at all cost" mentality |

Punishments vary depending on the severity of deviance. For example, a minor infringement such as a professional foul is often punished with a warning. Alternatively, taking drugs or fixing matches can result in a permanent ban or even a prison sentence.

Why do you think deviance is more common in elite-level sport?

daydream
EDUCATION

SPECTATOR BEHAVIOUR

Spectators can have positive and negative influences on sporting events.

+ Spectator attendance can raise extra funds for the sport.

+ Spectators can create a home-field advantage for the home team/individual.

+ An exciting atmosphere can enhance the experience for spectators.

− Spectators can cause increased pressure for players, which can negatively impact performance.

− Large crowds cause safety concerns and costs for the organisers.

− There is a danger of hostility and violence between opposing fans.

HOOLIGANISM

Hooliganism is disorderly, aggressive and often violent behaviour committed by spectators at sporting events. As well as causing physical harm, it can negatively affect participation numbers, and deter fans from attending events due to the threat of harm.

Causes:

- *Rivalries, e.g. between local teams*
- *Hype from the media*
- *Alcohol or drugs*
- *Gang culture*
- *Frustration, e.g. at an official's decision*
- *Peer pressure and perceived masculinity*

PREVENTION

The following strategies can be used to combat hooliganism.

- *Early kick-offs:* reduce the potential for alcohol consumption prior to an event
- *All-seater stadia:* improves safety and makes crowd control easier
- *Segregation of fans:* separates opposing fans, reducing the chance of violence
- *Improved security:* increases surveillance and the number of security staff at the event
- *Travel restrictions:* reduces potential for interactions between opposing fans
- *Education campaigns:* educate fans about the negative impacts of hooliganism

Many of these strategies incur a high cost so it is important to evaluate the effectiveness of each strategy in ensuring the safety of players and spectators.

49

PERFORMANCE-ENHANCING DRUGS

Performance-enhancing drugs can produce physical or psychological effects that improve performance. However, misuse of these drugs can pose significant health risks, and taking them is regarded as cheating.

BETA BLOCKERS

- Block the effects of adrenaline, lowering heart rate and blood pressure.
- Reduce muscle tension; improve fine motor control.
- Should be prescribed by a medical professional.
- Advantageous in precision sports such as snooker and archery.

Possible side effects: dangerously low heart rate, low blood pressure, dizziness, nausea, diarrhoea, insomnia, sleep disturbances and tiredness.

STIMULANTS

- Increase brain activity and enhance mental and physical alertness.
- Reduce fatigue and speed up reaction times.
- Advantageous in sports in which aggression is beneficial, such as boxing and rugby, and endurance events in which it can be difficult to stay focused for a long time, such as long-distance cycling.

Possible side effects: insomnia, irritability, anxiety, irregular heart rate, dehydration, high blood pressure and addiction.

ANABOLIC STEROIDS

- Mimic the effects of the male sex hormone testosterone, which promotes muscle growth.
- Allow performers to train harder for longer, which improves strength.
- Speed up recovery time.
- Advantageous in sports that require strength and power such as sprinting and weightlifting.

Possible side effects: aggression and mood swings, acne, high blood pressure, liver damage, heart and circulatory problems, infertility and death.

daydream
EDUCATION

NARCOTICS/ANALGESICS

- Temporarily reduce pain by depressing the central nervous system.
- Allow athletes to continue to compete whilst injured.
- Provide a sense of elation and being unbeatable.

Possible side effects: nausea, vomiting, constipation, low blood pressure, further damage to injury, addiction, and loss of concentration and coordination.

DIURETICS

- Increase the rate of urine production and reduce the amount of fluid in the body, which helps performers lose weight.
- Reduce the concentration or mask the presence of other banned substances in urine.
- Advantageous in sports that have weight limits, such as boxing and horse racing.

Possible side effects: dehydration, dizziness, muscle pains or cramps, headaches, nausea, exhaustion, heart failure and kidney damage.

PEPTIDE HORMONES

Naturally occurring hormones that facilitate muscle growth and the production of red blood cells.

Erythropoietin (EPO)
- Increases production of red blood cells and the delivery of oxygen to working muscles.
- Advantageous in sports that require endurance such as long-distance running or cycling.

Possible side effects: thickened blood, stroke, heart attack, blood clots and seizures.

Human Growth Hormone (HGH)
- Increases muscle mass and improves strength.
- Advantageous in sports that require strength and power such as sprinting.

Possible side effects: arthritis, heart failure, high cholesterol, high blood pressure and diabetes.

Blood doping involves increasing the number of red blood cells in the blood stream to boost its oxygen-carrying capacity and improve endurance. This is often done through blood transfusions. *Possible side effects: infection, heart attack, thickened blood and embolism (vessel blockage).*

Performers take PEDs to increase their chance of success, achieve fame/wealth, or to level the playing field with other competitors. However, PEDs can result in fines and bans, and damage the reputation and credibility of both the performer and the sport.

HEALTH, FITNESS & WELL-BEING

Health is a state of complete physical, mental and social wellbeing; not just the absence of disease or illness. Fitness is the ability to meet the demands of the environment.

PHYSICAL HEALTH

Health Benefits

Regular physical activity can improve physical health and reduce health risks.
Health benefits include:

- Improved heart function
- Improved efficiency of the body systems
- Ability to undertake everyday tasks
- Reduced risk of obesity and associated health problems, such as heart disease and diabetes

FITNESS

Fitness Benefits

Regular physical activity can also improve fitness levels and physical ability.
Fitness benefits include:

- Reduced chance of injury
- Greater ability to carry out physical work and everyday manual tasks

MENTAL HEALTH

Mental Benefits

Regular physical activity can help improve mental health and well-being.
Mental benefits include:

- Improved confidence and self-esteem
- Reduced risk of depression
- Relief from stress and tension
- Improved ability to deal with pressure and manage emotions
- Increased serotonin and endorphin levels, which help improve mood

SOCIAL HEALTH

Social Benefits

Regular physical activity can help improve social health.
Social benefits include:

- Essential human needs (food, shelter and clothing) are met
- Opportunities to socialise and make new friends
- Improved social and teamwork skills
- Learn to cooperate with others

Health and fitness are closely linked. Ill health can result in decreased fitness due to an inability to train. However, it is possible for a person to be unhealthy and still able to train.

daydream
EDUCATION

CONSEQUENCES OF A SEDENTARY LIFESTYLE

A sedentary lifestyle is a lifestyle that includes little or irregular physical activity and prolonged periods of time spent sitting.

CONSEQUENCES OF A SEDENTARY LIFESTYLE

- Gaining weight or becoming obese
- Heart disease
- Hypertension (high blood pressure)
- Diabetes
- Poor sleep or insomnia
- Lethargy or tiredness
- Poor self-esteem

OBESITY

An obese person is overweight and has extremely high body fat levels. Obesity can result from eating too much, a lack of physical activity and/or genetic factors. Obesity can lead to physical, mental and social health problems.

Physical	Mental	Social
- Cancer - Heart disease/heart attacks - Type 2 diabetes	- Depression - Loss of confidence	- Inability to socialise - Inability to leave the house

Being obese can have negative effects on a person's performance in physical activity and sport. It can limit:

Endurance	Excess weight can make it difficult to exercise for prolonged periods of time.	**Flexibility**	Excess fat around joints decreases the range of movement.
Speed/power	Excess weight makes moving quickly and strongly difficult.	**Agility**	Excess weight makes it hard to change direction quickly and accurately.

SOMATOTYPING

Body composition is the percentage of body weight that is fat, muscle and bone. Identifying body type is called **somatotyping**. There are three extreme somatotypes:

Extreme Endomorph

Wide hips
Pear-shaped body
Stores fat easily

Suited to activities that involve power, or where weight is advantageous (e.g. power-lifting and shot-put).

Extreme Mesomorph

Wide shoulders
Narrow hips
Builds muscle easily

Suited to activities that require strength, agility or speed (e.g. sprinting, hockey and boxing).

Extreme Ectomorph

Narrow shoulders
Narrow hips
Struggles to store fat and build muscle

Suited to endurance activities (e.g. long-distance running and cycling).

Most people lie somewhere in-between the extreme body types.

daydream EDUCATION

NUTRITION

A balanced diet consists of lots of different types of food to provide the suitable nutrients, vitamins and minerals needed by the body to grow and stay healthy.

A BALANCED DIET

The body needs nutrients for energy, growth and hydration. A balanced diet contains 55–60% carbohydrate, 25–30% fat and 15–20% protein.

CARBOHYDRATES	FATS	PROTEINS
55–60%	25–30%	15–20%

Carbohydrates

Carbohydrates are the body's main source of energy for all types and intensities of exercise. They should make up around 55–60% of a balanced diet.

 Simple carbs digest quickly and cause spikes in blood sugar and energy levels.

 Complex carbs digest slowly and keep blood sugar levels stable.

Fat

Fat is another energy source. It provides more energy than carbohydrates, but only at a low intensity. Fat should make up around 25–30% of a balanced diet.

 Saturated and trans fats increase cholesterol and the risk of heart disease, diabetes and other health problems.

 Not all fats are bad for you. **Good fats** can help lower cholesterol, reduce blood pressure and improve overall health.

Proteins

Protein is an essential nutrient that the body uses for growth and repair of muscle tissue. Protein should make up around 15–20% of a balanced diet.

 For some athletes, such as sprinters and weight-lifters, **protein** is important for building muscle.

daydream EDUCATION

ENERGY USE

The energy needed by your body comes from the air your breathe, the food you eat and the fluids you drink. Energy is measured in calories (Kcal). The average adult male requires 2,500 calories (Kcal) per day, whereas the average adult female requires 2,000 Kcal per day.

– Negative

If you eat less food than you need, your body will use up its fat reserves and you will lose weight.

Energy Balance

+ Positive

If you eat more food than you need, the surplus will be stored as fat and you will gain weight.

The number of calories you need depends on your age, gender, height and energy expenditure.

VITAMINS AND MINERALS

Vitamins and minerals are essential for maintaining the efficient working of the body systems and general health. Fruit and vegetables are packed full of vitamins and minerals.

Vitamin A is needed for good eyesight, growth and healthy skin and tissue.

Vitamin C helps protect the body from infections, heal wounds and absorb calcium and iron from food.

WATER

Water is essential for the body. It is involved in every bodily function and makes up over half of your body weight. A lack of water can lead to dehydration; an excessive loss of body water that interrupts the functioning of the body.

Dehydration can result in:

- *Blood thickening (increased viscosity), which slows blood flow*
- *An increased or irregular heart rate (rhythm)*
- *Increased body temperature, leading to overheating*
- *Increased reaction time, leading to poorer decisions*
- *Muscle fatigue, leading to muscle cramps*

Water balance (hydration) prevents dehydration.

USE OF DATA

Collecting relevant data and presenting it effectively can help performers monitor their progress, identify strengths and weaknesses and set targets.

Quantitative Data

Quantitative data has a numerical value and can be measured. It can be displayed in tables and graphs and analysed easily.

'It took 12.04 seconds for the athlete to finish the 100 m race', is an example of quantitative data.

Quantitative data can be collected via questionnaires and surveys.

Qualitative Data

Qualitative data is described using words and cannot be measured. It is often more difficult to analyse than quantitative data.

'The gymnast performed her routine exceptionally', is an example of qualitative data.

Qualitative data can be collected via observations and interviews.

PRESENTING DATA

Data is a series of observations, facts or statistics. Raw data can be difficult to understand and interpret. As a result, it is often organised in tables, graphs and charts.

Tables

Tables present raw data in rows and columns. They are precise and show all data.
This table shows the 10 km times of a runner during an 8-week training plan.

Week	1	2	3	4	5	6	7	8
Time	1:03.21	59.36	54.01	52.32	51.56	50.29	51.07	49.58

It can be difficult to interpret data in tables and to identify patterns.
As a result, data from tables is often presented in charts and graphs.

Bar Charts

A bar chart is used to display qualitative and categorical numerical data. Data is represented by different sized bars. The following bar chart shows how often students exercise in a week.

When drawing bar charts:

- Give the chart a title.
- Label both axes.
- Use equal intervals on the axes.
- Leave a gap between each bar.

How many times a week do students exercise?

Number of Students (y-axis, 0 to 25)
Number of Exercise Sessions a Week (x-axis, 0 to 7)

daydream
EDUCATION

Pie Charts

A pie chart is a circular chart that is split into sections to show proportion. The following pie charts display the BMIs of different age groups.

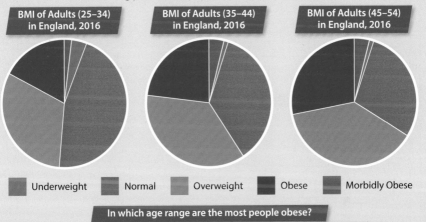

BMI of Adults (25–34) in England, 2016

BMI of Adults (35–44) in England, 2016

BMI of Adults (45–54) in England, 2016

Underweight   Normal   Overweight   Obese   Morbidly Obese

In which age range are the most people obese?

Line Graphs

Line graphs are used to display continuous data and help show trends or change over time. In a line graph, data is plotted as a series of points that are joined with straight lines. Always ensure that your line graph has a title and that the axes are labelled and use equal intervals.

This line graph shows how the TV rights revenue for premier league football has increased significantly over time, as a result of commercialisation.

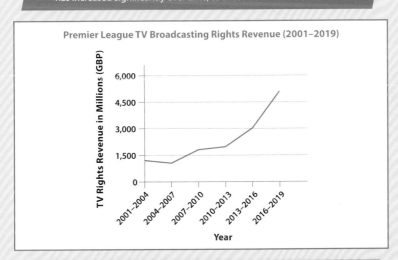

Premier League TV Broadcasting Rights Revenue (2001–2019)

How much revenue from TV rights was generated between 2013 and 2016?

Notes

Notes

Index

30-metre sprint test 32
Abdominals 10
Abduction 9, 20
Adduction 9, 20
Aerobic exercise 16-17, 34-35, 36
Age 46
Aggresion 45
Agility 23
Anabolic steroids 50
Anaerobic exercise 16-17, 34-35, 36
Analgesics 51
Antagonistic muscle pairs 11
Arousal 44
Axes of movement 20-21
Balance 24
Bar charts 56
Behaviour 48-49
Betablockers 50
Biceps 10
Blood 12,15, 51
Blood vessels 15
Bones 6-7
     long bones 7
     flat bones 7
     short bones 7
Breathing 13, 18
Carbohydrates 54
Carbon dioxide 16-17
Cardiac output 15
Cardiovascular endurance 25
Cardiovascular system 14-15
Circuit training 28, 34
Commercialisation 47
Continuous training 34
Cool down 27, 37, 39
Coordination 26
Cranium 6
Culture 46
Data 22, 23, 24, 25, 26, 27, 28, 29, 30, 31, 32, 56-57
Dehydration 55
Deltoid 10
Deviance 48
Diet 17, 54-55
Disability 46
Diuretics 51
Dorsi-flexion 9

Energy 16, 55
EPOC 17
Exercise 18
Extension 9, 20
Extroverts 45
Fartlek training 28, 34
Fat 53, 54
Feedback 42
Femur 6
Fibula 6
Fitness 22-32, 52
Fitness testing 22
FITT 33
Flexibility 27, 39
Flexion 9, 20
Gamesmanship 48
Gaseous exchange 12, 14
Gastrocnemius 10
Gender 46
Glucose 16
Gluteals 10
Goals and targets 41
Guidance 43
Hamstring 10
Hand grip dynometer test 31
Health 52
Heart 14, 18, 36
Heart rate 15, 18, 25, 36
High-altitude training 35
Hip flexors 10
Hooliganism 49
Humerus 6
Hydration 37
Illinois agility test 23
Information processing model 42
Interval training 32, 34
Introverts 45
Isometric muscle contractions 11
Isotonic muscle contractions 11
Joints 8-9
Key principles of overload 33
Kit 37
Lactic acid 16-17
Latissimus dorsi 10
Lever systems 19
Line graphs 57

Index

Media 47
Memory 42
Mental health 52
Mental preparation 39, 44
Minerals 7, 55
Motivation 44
Movement 7, 9, 11, 19, 20-21
Multi stage fitness test 25
Muscles 10, 11
Muscular endurance 28
Narcotics 51
Nutrition 54-55
Obesity 53
Overstretching 37
Overtraining 37
Oxygen 12-13, 14-15, 16-17
Participation 46
Patella 6
Pectorals 10
Pelvis 6
People 46
Peptide hormones 51
Performance-enhancing drugs 50-51
Personality 45
Pie charts 57
Planes of Movement 20-21
Plantar-flexion 9
Plyometrics training 29, 32, 35
Power 29, 32
Presenting data 56
Preventing injuries 37, 38
Prevention (hooliganism) 49
Principles of training 33
Progressive overload 33
Proteins 54
Quadriceps 10
Qualitative data 22, 56
Quantitative data 22, 56
Race 46
Radius 6
Reaction time 30
Recovery 17
Religion 46
Respiratory system 12-13
Rest 37
Reversibility 33

Ribs 6
Rotation 9, 20
Rotator cuffs 10
Ruler drop test 22, 30
Scapula 6
Sedentary lifestyle 53
Sit and reach test 27
Sit-up bleep test 28
Skeleton 6-7
Skills 26, 39, 40
SMART 41
Social health 52
Somatotypes 53
Specificity 33
Spectator behaviour 49
Speed 32, 34
Spirometer traces 13
Sponsorship 47
Sportsmanship 48
Static stretching 27, 35, 39
Sternum 6
Stimulants 50
Stork test 24
Strength 31, 32
Stress 44
Synovial joint 8
Tables 23-32, 56
Talus 6
Technique 37
Tedium 33
Tibia 6
Tibialis anterior 10
Training 33-36, 38
Training seasons 38
Training thresholds 25, 36
Training zones 25, 36
Triceps 10
Types of training 34-35
Ulna 6
Vertebrae 6
Vertical jump test 29
Vitamins 55
Wall toss test 26
Warm up 27, 37, 39
Water 16, 55
Weight training 28, 29, 31, 32, 35